The Beginning-Shell Scripting

INDEX

1. The Beginning- What is Shell?

A shell script is a computer program designed to be run by the Unix/Linux shell which could be one of the following:

- The Bourne Shell
- The C Shell
- The Korn Shell
- The GNU Bourne-Again Shell

A shell is a command-line interpreter and typical operations performed by shell scripts include file manipulation, program execution, and printing text.

Extended Shell Scripts

Shell scripts have several required constructs that tell the shell environment what to do and when to do it. Of course, most scripts are more complex than the above one.

The shell is, after all, a real programming language, complete with variables, control structures, and so forth. No matter how complicated a script gets, it is still just a list of commands executed sequentially.

The following script uses the **read** command which takes the input from the keyboard and assigns it as the value of the variable PERSON and finally prints it on STDOUT.

```
#!/bin/sh
```

```
# Author : Zara Ali

# Copyright (c) Tutorialspoint.com

# Script follows here:


echo "What is your name?"

read PERSON

echo "Hello, $PERSON"
```

Here is a sample run of the script −

```
$./test.sh

What is your name?

Zara Ali

Hello, Zara Ali

$
```

Subsequent part of this tutorial will cover Unix/Linux Shell Scripting in detail.

A **Shell** provides you with an interface to the Unix system. It gathers input from you and executes programs based on that input. When a program finishes executing, it displays that program's output.

Shell is an environment in which we can run our commands, programs, and shell scripts. There are different flavors of a shell, just as there are different flavors of operating systems. Each flavor of shell has its own set of recognized commands and functions.

Shell Prompt

The prompt, **$**, which is called the **command prompt**, is issued by the shell. While the prompt is displayed, you can type a command.

Shell reads your input after you press **Enter**. It determines the command you want executed by looking at the first word of your input. A word is an unbroken set of characters. Spaces and tabs separate words.

Following is a simple example of the **date** command, which displays the current date and time –

```
$date

Thu Jun 25 08:30:19 MST 2009
```

You can customize your command prompt using the environment variable PS1 explained in the Environment tutorial.

Shell Types

In Unix, there are two major types of shells –

- **Bourne shell** – If you are using a Bourne-type shell, the $ character is the default prompt.
- **C shell** – If you are using a C-type shell, the % character is the default prompt.

The Bourne Shell has the following subcategories –

- Bourne shell (sh)
- Korn shell (ksh)
- Bourne Again shell (bash)
- POSIX shell (sh)

The different C-type shells follow –

- C shell (csh)
- TENEX/TOPS C shell (tcsh)

The original Unix shell was written in the mid-1970s by Stephen R. Bourne while he was at the AT&T Bell Labs in New Jersey.

Bourne shell was the first shell to appear on Unix systems, thus it is referred to as "the shell".

Bourne shell is usually installed as **/bin/sh** on most versions of Unix. For this reason, it is the shell of choice for writing scripts that can be used on different versions of Unix.

In this chapter, we are going to cover most of the Shell concepts that are based on the Borne Shell.

Shell Scripts

The basic concept of a shell script is a list of commands, which are listed in the order of execution. A good shell script will have comments, preceded by # sign, describing the steps.

There are conditional tests, such as value A is greater than value B, loops allowing us to go through massive amounts of data, files to read and store data, and variables to read and store data, and the script may include functions.

We are going to write many scripts in the next sections. It would be a simple text file in which we would put all our commands and several other required constructs that tell the shell environment what to do and when to do it.

Shell scripts and functions are both interpreted. This means they are not compiled.

Example Script

Assume we create a **test.sh** script. Note all the scripts would have the **.sh** extension. Before you add anything else to your script, you need to alert the system that a shell script is being started. This is done using the **shebang** construct. For example –

```
#!/bin/sh
```

This tells the system that the commands that follow are to be executed by the Bourne shell. *It's called a shebang because the # symbol is called a hash, and the ! symbol is called a bang.*

To create a script containing these commands, you put the shebang line first and then add the commands –

```
#!/bin/bash

pwd

ls
```

Shell Comments

You can put your comments in your script as follows –

```
#!/bin/bash



# Author : Zara Ali

# Copyright (c) Tutorialspoint.com

# Script follows here:

pwd

ls
```

Save the above content and make the script executable –

```
$chmod +x test.sh
```

The shell script is now ready to be executed –

$./test.sh

Upon execution, you will receive the following result –

/home/amrood

index.htm unix-basic_utilities.htm unix-directories.htm

test.sh unix-communication.htm unix-environment.htm

Note – To execute a program available in the current directory, use **./program_name**

Extended Shell Scripts

Shell scripts have several required constructs that tell the shell environment what to do and when to do it. Of course, most scripts are more complex than the above one.

The shell is, after all, a real programming language, complete with variables, control structures, and so forth. No matter how complicated a script gets, it is still just a list of commands executed sequentially.

The following script uses the **read** command which takes the input from the keyboard and assigns it as the value of the variable PERSON and finally prints it on STDOUT.

```
#!/bin/sh


# Author : Zara Ali

# Copyright (c) Tutorialspoint.com

# Script follows here:


echo "What is your name?"

read PERSON

echo "Hello, $PERSON"
```

Here is a sample run of the script −

$./test.sh

What is your name?

Zara Ali

Hello, Zara Ali$

2. Shell Variables

In this chapter, we will learn how to use Shell variables in Unix. A variable is a character string to which we assign a value. The value assigned could be a number, text, filename, device, or any other type of data.

A variable is nothing more than a pointer to the actual data. The shell enables you to create, assign, and delete variables.

Variable Names

The name of a variable can contain only letters (a to z or A to Z), numbers (0 to 9) or the underscore character (_).

By convention, Unix shell variables will have their names in UPPERCASE.

The following examples are valid variable names –

_ALI

TOKEN_A

VAR_1

VAR_2

Following are the examples of invalid variable names –

2_VAR

-VARIABLE

VAR1-VAR2

VAR_A!

The reason you cannot use other characters such as !, *, or - is that these characters have a special meaning for the shell.

Defining Variables

Variables are defined as follows −

variable_name=variable_value

For example −

```
NAME="Zara Ali"
```

The above example defines the variable NAME and assigns the value "Zara Ali" to it. Variables of this type are called **scalar variables**. A scalar variable can hold only one value at a time.

Shell enables you to store any value you want in a variable. For example −

```
VAR1="Zara Ali"

VAR2=100
```

To access the value stored in a variable, prefix its name with the dollar sign ($) –

For example, the following script will access the value of defined variable NAME and print it on STDOUT –

```
#!/bin/sh

NAME="Zara Ali"

echo $NAME
```

The above script will produce the following value –

Zara Ali

Read-only Variables

Shell provides a way to mark variables as read-only by using the read-only command. After a variable is marked read-only, its value cannot be changed.

For example, the following script generates an error while trying to change the value of NAME –

```
#!/bin/sh
```

```
NAME="Zara Ali"

readonly NAME

NAME="Qadiri"
```

The above script will generate the following result –

/bin/sh: NAME: This variable is read only.

Unsetting Variables

Unsetting or deleting a variable directs the shell to remove the variable from the list of variables that it tracks. Once you unset a variable, you cannot access the stored value in the variable.

Following is the syntax to unset a defined variable using the **unset** command –

```
unset variable_name
```

The above command unsets the value of a defined variable. Here is a simple example that demonstrates how the command works –

```
#!/bin/sh


NAME="Zara Ali"
```

```
unset NAME

echo $NAME
```

The above example does not print anything. You cannot use the unset command to **unset** variables that are marked **readonly**.

Variable Types

When a shell is running, three main types of variables are present –

- **Local Variables** – A local variable is a variable that is present within the current instance of the shell. It is not available to programs that are started by the shell. They are set at the command prompt.
- **Environment Variables** – An environment variable is available to any child process of the shell. Some programs need environment variables in order to function correctly. Usually, a shell script defines only those environment variables that are needed by the programs that it runs.
- **Shell Variables** – A shell variable is a special variable that is set by the shell and is required by the shell in order to function correctly. Some of these variables are environment variables whereas others are local variables.

3. Special Variables

In this chapter, we will discuss in detail about special variable in Unix. In one of our previous chapters, we understood how to be careful when we use certain nonalphanumeric characters in variable names. This is because those characters are used in the names of special Unix variables. These variables are reserved for specific functions.

For example, the **$** character represents the process ID number, or PID, of the current shell –

```
$echo $$
```

The above command writes the PID of the current shell –

29949

The following table shows a number of special variables that you can use in your shell scripts –

Sr.No.	Variable & Description
1	**$0** The filename of the current script.
2	**$n** These variables correspond to the arguments with which a script was invoked. Here **n** is a positive decimal number corresponding to the position of

	an argument (the first argument is $1, the second argument is $2, and so on).
3	**$#** The number of arguments supplied to a script.
4	**$*** All the arguments are double quoted. If a script receives two arguments, $* is equivalent to $1 $2.
5	**$@** All the arguments are individually double quoted. If a script receives two arguments, $@ is equivalent to $1 $2.
6	**$?** The exit status of the last command executed.
7	**$$** The process number of the current shell. For shell scripts, this is the process ID under which they are executing.
8	**$!** The process number of the last background command.

Command-Line Arguments

The command-line arguments $1, $2, $3, ...$9 are positional parameters, with $0 pointing to the actual command, program, shell script, or function and $1, $2, $3, ...$9 as the arguments to the command.

Following script uses various special variables related to the command line –

```
#!/bin/sh


echo "File Name: $0"

echo "First Parameter : $1"

echo "Second Parameter : $2"

echo "Quoted Values: $@"

echo "Quoted Values: $*"

echo "Total Number of Parameters : $#"
```

Here is a sample run for the above script –

$./test.sh Zara Ali

File Name : ./test.sh

First Parameter : Zara

Second Parameter : Ali

Quoted Values: Zara Ali

Quoted Values: Zara Ali

Total Number of Parameters : 2

Special Parameters $* and $@

There are special parameters that allow accessing all the command-line arguments at once. **$*** and **$@** both will act the same unless they are enclosed in double quotes, "".

Both the parameters specify the command-line arguments. However, the "$*" special parameter takes the entire list as one argument with spaces between and the "$@" special parameter takes the entire list and separates it into separate arguments.

We can write the shell script as shown below to process an unknown number of commandline arguments with either the $* or $@ special parameters –

```
#!/bin/sh


for TOKEN in $*

do

   echo $TOKEN

done
```

Here is a sample run for the above script –

```
$./test.sh Zara Ali 10 Years Old

Zara
```

Ali

10

Years

Old

Note – Here **do...done** is a kind of loop that will be covered in a subsequent tutorial.

Exit Status

The **$?** variable represents the exit status of the previous command.

Exit status is a numerical value returned by every command upon its completion. As a rule, most commands return an exit status of 0 if they were successful, and 1 if they were unsuccessful.

Some commands return additional exit statuses for particular reasons. For example, some commands differentiate between kinds of errors and will return various exit values depending on the specific type of failure.

Following is the example of successful command –

$./test.sh Zara Ali

File Name : ./test.sh

First Parameter : Zara

Second Parameter : Ali

Quoted Values: Zara Ali

Quoted Values: Zara Ali

Total Number of Parameters : 2

$echo $?

0

$

4. Shell Arrays

In this chapter, we will discuss how to use shell arrays in Unix. A shell variable is capable enough to hold a single value. These variables are called scalar variables.

Shell supports a different type of variable called an **array variable**. This can hold multiple values at the same time. Arrays provide a method of grouping a set of variables. Instead of creating a new name for each variable that is required, you can use a single array variable that stores all the other variables.

All the naming rules discussed for Shell Variables would be applicable while naming arrays.

Defining Array Values

The difference between an array variable and a scalar variable can be explained as follows.

Suppose you are trying to represent the names of various students as a set of variables. Each of the individual variables is a scalar variable as follows –

```
NAME01="Zara"

NAME02="Qadir"

NAME03="Mahnaz"

NAME04="Ayan"
```

```
NAME05="Daisy"
```

We can use a single array to store all the above mentioned names. Following is the simplest method of creating an array variable. This helps assign a value to one of its indices.

array_name[index]=value

Here *array_name* is the name of the array, *index* is the index of the item in the array that you want to set, and value is the value you want to set for that item.

As an example, the following commands −

```
NAME[0]="Zara"

NAME[1]="Qadir"

NAME[2]="Mahnaz"

NAME[3]="Ayan"

NAME[4]="Daisy"
```

If you are using the **ksh** shell, here is the syntax of array initialization −

set -A array_name value1 value2 ... valuen

If you are using the **bash** shell, here is the syntax of array initialization −

array_name=(value1 ... valuen)

Accessing Array Values

After you have set any array variable, you access it as follows −

${array_name[index]}

Here *array_name* is the name of the array, and *index* is the index of the value to be accessed. Following is an example to understand the concept −

```
#!/bin/sh


NAME[0]="Zara"

NAME[1]="Qadir"

NAME[2]="Mahnaz"

NAME[3]="Ayan"

NAME[4]="Daisy"

echo "First Index: ${NAME[0]}"

echo "Second Index: ${NAME[1]}"
```

The above example will generate the following result –

```
$./test.sh

First Index: Zara

Second Index: Qadir
```

You can access all the items in an array in one of the following ways –

```
${array_name[*]}

${array_name[@]}
```

Here **array_name** is the name of the array you are interested in. Following example will help you understand the concept –

```
#!/bin/sh


NAME[0]="Zara"

NAME[1]="Qadir"

NAME[2]="Mahnaz"

NAME[3]="Ayan"
```

```
NAME[4]="Daisy"

echo "First Method: ${NAME[*]}"

echo "Second Method: ${NAME[@]}"
```

The above example will generate the following result –

```
$./test.sh

First Method: Zara Qadir Mahnaz Ayan Daisy

Second Method: Zara Qadir Mahnaz Ayan Daisy
```

5. Basic Operators

There are various operators supported by each shell. We will discuss in detail about Bourne shell (default shell) in this chapter.

We will now discuss the following operators –

- Arithmetic Operators
- Relational Operators
- Boolean Operators
- String Operators
- File Test Operators

Bourne shell didn't originally have any mechanism to perform simple arithmetic operations but it uses external programs, either **awk** or **expr**.

The following example shows how to add two numbers –

```
#!/bin/sh



val=`expr 2 + 2`

echo "Total value : $val"
```

The above script will generate the following result –

Total value : 4

The following points need to be considered while adding

–

- There must be spaces between operators and expressions. For example, 2+2 is not correct; it should be written as 2 + 2.
- The complete expression should be enclosed between ‘ ‘, called the backtick.

Arithmetic Operators

The following arithmetic operators are supported by Bourne Shell.

Assume variable **a** holds 10 and variable **b** holds 20 then

–

It is very important to understand that all the conditional expressions should be inside square braces with spaces around them, for example **[$a == $b]** is correct whereas, **[$a==$b]** is incorrect.

All the arithmetical calculations are done using long integers.

Example

Here is an example which uses all the arithmetic operators

–

```
#!/bin/sh


a=10

b=20


val=`expr $a + $b`

echo "a + b : $val"


val=`expr $a - $b`

echo "a - b : $val"


val=`expr $a \* $b`

echo "a * b : $val"


val=`expr $b / $a`

echo "b / a : $val"
```

```
val=`expr $b % $a`
echo "b % a : $val"


if [ $a == $b ]
then
  echo "a is equal to b"
fi


if [ $a != $b ]
then
  echo "a is not equal to b"
fi
```

The above script will produce the following result –

a + b : 30

a - b : -10

a * b : 200

b / a : 2

b % a : 0

a is not equal to b

The following points need to be considered when using the Arithmetic Operators –

- There must be spaces between the operators and the expressions. For example, 2+2 is not correct; it should be written as 2 + 2.
- Complete expression should be enclosed between ' ', called the inverted commas.
- You should use \ on the * symbol for multiplication.
- **if...then...fi** statement is a decision-making statement which has been explained in the next chapter.

Operator	Description	Example
+ (Addition)	Adds values on either side of the operator	\`expr $a + $b\` will give 30
- (Subtraction)	Subtracts right hand operand from left hand operand	\`expr $a - $b\` will give -10
* (Multiplication)	Multiplies values on either side of the operator	\`expr $a \* $b\` will give 200

/ (Division)	Divides left hand operand by right hand operand	`expr $b / $a` will give 2
% (Modulus)	Divides left hand operand by right hand operand and returns remainder	`expr $b % $a` will give 0
= (Assignment)	Assigns right operand in left operand	a = $b would assign value of b into a
== (Equality)	Compares two numbers, if both are same then returns true.	[$a == $b] would return false.
!= (Not Equality)	Compares two numbers, if both are different then returns true.	[$a != $b] would return true.

It is very important to understand that all the conditional expressions should be inside square braces with spaces around them, for example **[$a == $b]** is correct whereas, **[$a==$b]** is incorrect.

All the arithmetical calculations are done using long integers.

Relational Operators

Bourne Shell supports the following relational operators that are specific to numeric values. These operators do not work for string values unless their value is numeric.

For example, following operators will work to check a relation between 10 and 20 as well as in between "10" and "20" but not in between "ten" and "twenty".

Assume variable **a** holds 10 and variable **b** holds 20 then −

It is very important to understand that all the conditional expressions should be placed inside square braces with spaces around them. For example, **[$a <= $b]** is correct whereas, **[$a <= $b]** is incorrect.

Example

Here is an example which uses all the relational operators −

```
#!/bin/sh

a=10

b=20

```

```
if [ $a -eq $b ]

then

  echo "$a -eq $b : a is equal to b"

else

  echo "$a -eq $b: a is not equal to b"

fi


if [ $a -ne $b ]

then

  echo "$a -ne $b: a is not equal to b"

else

  echo "$a -ne $b : a is equal to b"

fi


if [ $a -gt $b ]

then

  echo "$a -gt $b: a is greater than b"
```

```
else
  echo "$a -gt $b: a is not greater than b"
fi

if [ $a -lt $b ]
then
  echo "$a -lt $b: a is less than b"
else
  echo "$a -lt $b: a is not less than b"
fi

if [ $a -ge $b ]
then
  echo "$a -ge $b: a is greater or  equal to b"
else
  echo "$a -ge $b: a is not greater or equal to b"
fi
```

```
if [ $a -le $b ]
then
   echo "$a -le $b: a is less or  equal to b"
else
   echo "$a -le $b: a is not less or equal to b"
fi
```

The above script will generate the following result −

```
10 -eq 20: a is not equal to b
10 -ne 20: a is not equal to b
10 -gt 20: a is not greater than b
10 -lt 20: a is less than b
10 -ge 20: a is not greater or equal to b
10 -le 20: a is less or  equal to b
```

The following points need to be considered while working with relational operators −

- There must be spaces between the operators and the expressions. For example, 2+2 is not correct; it should be written as 2 + 2.
- **if...then...else...fi** statement is a decision-making statement which has been explained in the next chapter.

Operator	Description	Example
-eq	Checks if the value of two operands are equal or not; if yes, then the condition becomes true.	[$a -eq $b] is not true.
-ne	Checks if the value of two operands are equal or not; if values are not equal, then the condition becomes true.	[$a -ne $b] is true.
-gt	Checks if the value of left operand is greater than the value of right operand; if yes, then the condition becomes true.	[$a -gt $b] is not true.
-lt	Checks if the value of left operand is less than the value of right operand; if yes, then the condition becomes true.	[$a -lt $b] is true.
-ge	Checks if the value of left operand is greater than or equal to the value of right operand; if yes, then the condition becomes true.	[$a -ge $b] is not true.

-le	Checks if the value of left operand is less than or equal to the value of right operand; if yes, then the condition becomes true.	[$a -le $b] is true.

It is very important to understand that all the conditional expressions should be placed inside square braces with spaces around them. For example, **[$a <= $b]** is correct whereas, **[$a <= $b]** is incorrect.

Boolean Operators

The following Boolean operators are supported by the Bourne Shell.

Assume variable **a** holds 10 and variable **b** holds 20 then

–

Example

Here is an example which uses all the Boolean operators

–

```
#!/bin/sh

a=10

b=20
```

```
if [ $a != $b ]

then

  echo "$a != $b : a is not equal to b"

else

  echo "$a != $b: a is equal to b"

fi



if [ $a -lt 100 -a $b -gt 15 ]

then

  echo "$a -lt 100 -a $b -gt 15 : returns true"

else

  echo "$a -lt 100 -a $b -gt 15 : returns false"

fi



if [ $a -lt 100 -o $b -gt 100 ]

then
```

```
  echo "$a -lt 100 -o $b -gt 100 : returns true"

else

  echo "$a -lt 100 -o $b -gt 100 : returns false"

fi



if [ $a -lt 5 -o $b -gt 100 ]

then

  echo "$a -lt 100 -o $b -gt 100 : returns true"

else

  echo "$a -lt 100 -o $b -gt 100 : returns false"

fi
```

The above script will generate the following result –

10 != 20 : a is not equal to b

10 -lt 100 -a 20 -gt 15 : returns true

10 -lt 100 -o 20 -gt 100 : returns true

10 -lt 5 -o 20 -gt 100 : returns false

The following points need to be considered while using the operators −

- There must be spaces between the operators and the expressions. For example, 2+2 is not correct; it should be written as 2 + 2.
- **if...then...else...fi** statement is a decision-making statement which has been explained in the next chapter.

Operator	Description	Example
!	This is logical negation. This inverts a true condition into false and vice versa.	[! false] is true.
-o	This is logical **OR**. If one of the operands is true, then the condition becomes true.	[$a -lt 20 -o $b -gt 100] is true.
-a	This is logical **AND**. If both the operands are true, then the condition becomes true otherwise false.	[$a -lt 20 -a $b -gt 100] is false.

String Operators

The following string operators are supported by Bourne Shell.

Assume variable **a** holds "abc" and variable **b** holds "efg" then −

Example

Here is an example which uses all the string operators −

```
#!/bin/sh

a="abc"
b="efg"

if [ $a = $b ]
then
   echo "$a = $b : a is equal to b"
else
   echo "$a = $b: a is not equal to b"
fi

if [ $a != $b ]
then
```

```
  echo "$a != $b : a is not equal to b"
else
  echo "$a != $b: a is equal to b"
fi

if [ -z $a ]
then
  echo "-z $a : string length is zero"
else
  echo "-z $a : string length is not zero"
fi

if [ -n $a ]
then
  echo "-n $a : string length is not zero"
else
  echo "-n $a : string length is zero"
```

```
fi


if [ $a ]

then

   echo "$a : string is not empty"

else

   echo "$a : string is empty"

fi
```

The above script will generate the following result −

abc = efg: a is not equal to b

abc != efg : a is not equal to b

-z abc : string length is not zero

-n abc : string length is not zero

abc : string is not empty

The following points need to be considered while using the operator −

- There must be spaces between the operators and the expressions. For example, 2+2 is not correct. It should be written as 2 + 2.
- **if...then...else...fi** statement is a decision-making statement which has been explained in the next chapter.

Operator	Description	Example
=	Checks if the value of two operands are equal or not; if yes, then the condition becomes true.	[$a = $b] is not true.
!=	Checks if the value of two operands are equal or not; if values are not equal then the condition becomes true.	[$a != $b] is true.
-z	Checks if the given string operand size is zero; if it is zero length, then it returns true.	[-z $a] is not true.
-n	Checks if the given string operand size is non-zero; if it is nonzero length, then it returns true.	[-n $a] is not false.
str	Checks if **str** is not the empty string; if it is empty, then it returns false.	[$a] is not false.

File Test Operators

We have a few operators that can be used to test various properties associated with a Unix file.

Assume a variable **file** holds an existing file name "test" the size of which is 100 bytes and has **read**, **write** and **execute** permission on −

Example

The following example uses all the **file test** operators −

Assume a variable file holds an existing file name **"/var/www/tutorialspoint/unix/test.sh"** the size of which is 100 bytes and has **read**, **write** and **execute** permission −

```
#!/bin/sh


file="/var/www/tutorialspoint/unix/test.sh"


if [ -r $file ]

then

  echo "File has read access"

else

  echo "File does not have read access"

fi
```

```
if [ -w $file ]
then
  echo "File has write permission"
else
  echo "File does not have write permission"
fi

if [ -x $file ]
then
  echo "File has execute permission"
else
  echo "File does not have execute permission"
fi

if [ -f $file ]
then
```

```
  echo "File is an ordinary file"
else
  echo "This is sepcial file"
fi


if [ -d $file ]
then
  echo "File is a directory"
else
  echo "This is not a directory"
fi


if [ -s $file ]
then
  echo "File size is not zero"
else
  echo "File size is zero"
```

```
fi


if [ -e $file ]
then
  echo "File exists"
else
  echo "File does not exist"
fi
```

The above script will produce the following result −

The file does not have written permission

The file does not have execution permission

This is special file

This is not a directory

The file size is not zero

The file does not exist

The following points need to be considered while using file test operators −

- There must be spaces between the operators and the expressions. For example, 2+2 is not correct; it should be written as 2 + 2.
- **if...then...else...fi** statement is a decision-making statement which has been explained in the next chapter.

Operator	Description	Example
-b file	Checks if file is a block special file; if yes, then the condition becomes true.	[-b $file] is false.
-c file	Checks if file is a character special file; if yes, then the condition becomes true.	[-c $file] is false.
-d file	Checks if file is a directory; if yes, then the condition becomes true.	[-d $file] is not true.
-f file	Checks if file is an ordinary file as opposed to a directory or special file; if yes, then the condition becomes true.	[-f $file] is true.
-g file	Checks if file has its set group ID (SGID) bit set; if yes, then the condition becomes true.	[-g $file] is false.
-k file	Checks if file has its sticky bit set; if yes, then the condition becomes true.	[-k $file] is false.
-p file	Checks if file is a named pipe; if yes, then the condition becomes true.	[-p $file] is false.
-t file	Checks if file descriptor is open and associated with a	[-t $file] is false.

	terminal; if yes, then the condition becomes true.	
-u file	Checks if file has its Set User ID (SUID) bit set; if yes, then the condition becomes true.	[-u $file] is false.
-r file	Checks if file is readable; if yes, then the condition becomes true.	[-r $file] is true.
-w file	Checks if file is writable; if yes, then the condition becomes true.	[-w $file] is true.
-x file	Checks if file is executable; if yes, then the condition becomes true.	[-x $file] is true.
-s file	Checks if file has size greater than 0; if yes, then condition becomes true.	[-s $file] is true.
-e file	Checks if file exists; is true even if file is a directory but exists.	[-e $file] is true.

C Shell Operators

We will now list down all the operators available in C Shell. Here most of the operators are very similar to what we have in C Programming language.

Operators are listed in the order of decreasing precedence –

Arithmetic and Logical Operators

The following table lists out a few Arithmetic and Logical Operators –

Sr.No.	Operator & Description
1	**()** Change precedence
2	**~** 1's complement
3	**!** Logical negation
4	***** Multiply
5	**/** Divide
6	**%** Modulo
7	**+** Add
8	**-** Subtract
9	**<<** Left shift
10	**>>** Right shift
11	**==** String comparison for equality
12	**!=** String comparison for non equality
13	**=~** Pattern matching
14	**&**

<table>
<tr><td></td><td>Bitwise "and"</td></tr>
<tr><td>15</td><td>^
Bitwise "exclusive or"</td></tr>
<tr><td>16</td><td>|
Bitwise "inclusive or"</td></tr>
<tr><td>17</td><td>**&&**
Logical "and"</td></tr>
<tr><td>18</td><td>||
Logical "or"</td></tr>
<tr><td>19</td><td>++
Increment</td></tr>
<tr><td>20</td><td>--
Decrement</td></tr>
<tr><td>21</td><td>=
Assignment</td></tr>
<tr><td>22</td><td>*=
Multiply left side by right side and update left side</td></tr>
<tr><td>23</td><td>/=
Divide left side by right side and update left side</td></tr>
<tr><td>24</td><td>+=
Add left side to right side and update left side</td></tr>
<tr><td>25</td><td>-=
Subtract left side from right side and update left side</td></tr>
<tr><td>26</td><td>^=
"Exclusive or" left side to right side and update left side</td></tr>
<tr><td>27</td><td>%=
Divide left by right side and update left side with remainder</td></tr>
</table>

File Test Operators

The following operators test various properties associated with a Unix file.

Sr.No.	Operator & Description
1	**-r file** Checks if file is readable; if yes, then the condition becomes true.
2	**-w file** Checks if file is writable; if yes, then the condition becomes true.
3	**-x file** Checks if file is executable; if yes, then the condition becomes true.
4	**-f file** Checks if file is an ordinary file as opposed to a directory or special file; if yes, then the condition becomes true.
5	**-z file** Checks if file has size greater than 0; if yes, then the condition becomes true.
6	**-d file** Checks if file is a directory; if yes, then the condition becomes true.
7	**-e file** Checks if file exists; is true even if file is a directory but exists.
8	**-o file** Checks if user owns the file; returns true if the user is the owner of the file.

Korn Shell Operators

We will now discuss all the operators available in Korn Shell. Most of the operators are very similar to what we have in the C Programming language.

Operators are listed in the order of decreasing precedence –

Arithmetic and Logical Operators

Sr.No.	Operator & Description
1	+ Unary plus
2	- Unary minus
3	!~ Logical negation; binary inversion (one's complement)
4	* Multiply
5	/ Divide
6	% Modulo
7	+ Add
8	- Subtract
9	<< Left shift
10	>> Right shift

<table>
<tr><td>11</td><td>==
String comparison for equality</td></tr>
<tr><td>12</td><td>!=
String comparison for non-equality</td></tr>
<tr><td>13</td><td>=~
Pattern matching</td></tr>
<tr><td>14</td><td>&
Bitwise "and"</td></tr>
<tr><td>15</td><td>^
Bitwise "exclusive or"</td></tr>
<tr><td>16</td><td>|
Bitwise "inclusive or"</td></tr>
<tr><td>17</td><td>&&
Logical "and"</td></tr>
<tr><td>18</td><td>||
Logical "or"</td></tr>
<tr><td>19</td><td>++
Increment</td></tr>
<tr><td>20</td><td>--
Decrement</td></tr>
<tr><td>21</td><td>=
Assignment</td></tr>
</table>

File Test Operators

The following operators test various properties associated with a Unix file.

Sr.No.	Operator & Description
1	**-r file** Checks if file is readable; if yes, then the condition becomes true.
2	**-w file**

	Checks if file is writable; if yes, then the condition becomes true.
3	**-x file** Checks if file is executable; if yes, then the condition becomes true.
4	**-f file** Checks if file is an ordinary file as opposed to a directory or special file; if yes, then the condition becomes true.
5	**-s file** Checks if file has size greater than 0; if yes, then the condition becomes true.
6	**-d file** Checks if file is a directory; if yes, then the condition becomes true.
7	**-e file** Checks if file exists; is true even if file is a directory but exists.

6. Decision Making

In this chapter, we will understand shell decision-making in Unix. While writing a shell script, there may be a situation when you need to adopt one path out of the given two paths. So you need to make use of conditional statements that allow your program to make correct decisions and perform the right actions.

Unix Shell supports conditional statements which are used to perform different actions based on different conditions. We will now understand two decision-making statements here −

- The **if...else** statement
- The **case...esac** statement

The if...else statements

If else statements are useful decision-making statements that can be used to select an option from a given set of options.

Unix Shell supports the following forms of **if…else** statements −

- **if...fi statement**

The **if...fi** statement is the fundamental control statement that allows Shell to make decisions and execute statements conditionally.

Syntax

```
if [ expression ]

then

   Statement(s) to be executed if expression is true

fi
```

The *Shell expression* is evaluated in the above syntax. If the resulting value is *true*, given *statement(s)* are executed. If the *expression* is *false* then no statement would be executed. Most of the times, comparison operators are used for making decisions.

It is recommended to be careful with the spaces between braces and expression. No space produces a syntax error.

If **expression** is a shell command, then it will be assumed true if it returns **0** after execution. If it is a Boolean expression, then it would be true if it returns true.

Example

```
#!/bin/sh

a=10
b=20

if [ $a == $b ]
then
   echo "a is equal to b"
fi
```

```
if [ $a != $b ]
then
  echo "a is not equal to b"
fi
```

The above script will generate the following result −

a is not equal to b

- **if...else...fi statement**

The **if...else...fi** statement is the next form of control statement that allows Shell to execute statements in a controlled way and make the right choice.

Syntax

if [expression]

then

  Statement(s) to be executed if expression is true

else

Statement(s) to be executed if expression is not true

fi

The Shell *expression* is evaluated in the above syntax. If the resulting value is *true*, given *statement(s)* are executed. If the *expression* is *false*, then no statement will be executed.

Example

The above example can also be written using the *if...else* statement as follows −

```
#!/bin/sh

a=10

b=20

if [ $a == $b ]

then

   echo "a is equal to b"

else
```

```
  echo "a is not equal to b"

fi
```

Upon execution, you will receive the following result −

a is not equal to b

- **if...elif...else...fi statement**

The **if...elif...fi** statement is the one level advance form of control statement that allows Shell to make correct decision out of several conditions.

Syntax

if [expression 1]

then

Statement(s) to be executed if expression 1 is true

elif [expression 2]

then

Statement(s) to be executed if expression 2 is true

```
elif [ expression 3 ]

then

   Statement(s) to be executed if expression 3 is true

else

   Statement(s) to be executed if no expression is true

fi
```

This code is just a series of *if* statements, where each *if* is part of the *else* clause of the previous statement. Here statement(s) are executed based on the true condition, if none of the condition is true then *else* block is executed.

Example

```
#!/bin/sh


a=10

b=20


if [ $a == $b ]
```

```
then
  echo "a is equal to b"
elif [ $a -gt $b ]
then
  echo "a is greater than b"
elif [ $a -lt $b ]
then
  echo "a is less than b"
else
  echo "None of the condition met"
fi
```

Upon execution, you will receive the following result –

a is less than b

Most of the if statements check relations using relational operators discussed in the previous chapter.

- **The case...esac Statement**

You can use multiple **if...elif** statements to perform a multiway branch. However, this is not always the best solution, especially when all of the branches depend on the value of a single variable.

Unix Shell supports **case...esac** statement which handles exactly this situation, and it does so more efficiently than repeated **if...elif** statements.

You can use multiple **if...elif** statements to perform a multiway branch. However, this is not always the best solution, especially when all of the branches depend on the value of a single variable.

Shell supports **case...esac** statement which handles exactly this situation, and it does so more efficiently than repeated if...elif statements.

Syntax

The basic syntax of the **case...esac** statement is to give an expression to evaluate and to execute several different statements based on the value of the expression.

The interpreter checks each case against the value of the expression until a match is found. If nothing matches, a default condition will be used.

```
case word in

  pattern1)
```

```
  Statement(s) to be executed if pattern1 matches

  ;;

pattern2)

  Statement(s) to be executed if pattern2 matches

  ;;

pattern3)

  Statement(s) to be executed if pattern3 matches

  ;;

*)

  Default condition to be executed

  ;;

esac
```

Here the string word is compared against every pattern until a match is found. The statement(s) following the matching pattern executes. If no matches are found, the case statement exits without performing any action.

There is no maximum number of patterns, but the minimum is one.

When statement(s) part executes, the command ;; indicates that the program flow should jump to the end of the entire case statement. This is similar to break in the C programming language.

Example

```
#!/bin/sh

FRUIT="kiwi"

case "$FRUIT" in
  "apple") echo "Apple pie is quite tasty."
  ;;
  "banana") echo "I like banana nut bread."
  ;;
  "kiwi") echo "New Zealand is famous for kiwi."
  ;;
```

```
esac
```

Upon execution, you will receive the following result −

New Zealand is famous for kiwi.

A good use for a case statement is the evaluation of command line arguments as follows −

```
#!/bin/sh


option="${1}"

case ${option} in

  -f) FILE="${2}"

    echo "File name is $FILE"

    ;;

  -d) DIR="${2}"

    echo "Dir name is $DIR"

    ;;

  *)

    echo "`basename ${0}`:usage: [-f file] | [-d directory]"
```

```
        exit 1 # Command to come out of the program with status 1
        ;;
    esac
```

Here is a sample run of the above program −

```
$./test.sh

test.sh: usage: [ -f filename ] | [ -d directory ]

$ ./test.sh -f index.htm

$ vi test.sh

$ ./test.sh -f index.htm

File name is index.htm

$ ./test.sh -d unix

Dir name is unix

$
```

The **case...esac** statement in the Unix shell is very similar to the **switch...case** statement we have in other programming languages like **C** or **C++** and **PERL**, etc.

7. Loop Types

In this chapter, we will discuss shell loops in Unix. A loop is a powerful programming tool that enables you to execute a set of commands repeatedly. In this chapter, we will examine the following types of loops available to shell programmers −

- **The while loop**

The **while** loop enables you to execute a set of commands repeatedly until some condition occurs. It is usually used when you need to manipulate the value of a variable repeatedly.

Syntax

```
while command

do

   Statement(s) to be executed if command is true

done
```

Here the Shell *command* is evaluated. If the resulting value is *true*, given *statement(s)* are executed. If *command* is *false* then no statement will be executed and the program will jump to the next line after the done statement.

Example

Here is a simple example that uses the **while** loop to display the numbers zero to nine –

```
#!/bin/sh

a=0

while [ $a -lt 10 ]
```

```
do
   echo $a
   a=`expr $a + 1`
done
```

Upon execution, you will receive the following result −

```
0
1
2
3
4
5
6
7
8
9
```

Each time this loop executes, the variable **a** is checked to see whether it has a value that is less than 10. If the value of **a** is less than 10, this test condition has an exit status of 0. In this case, the current value of **a** is displayed and later **a** is incremented by 1.

- **The for loop**

The **for** loop operates on lists of items. It repeats a set of commands for every item in a list.

Syntax

for var in word1 word2 ... wordN

do

Statement(s) to be executed for every word.

done

Here *var* is the name of a variable and word1 to wordN are sequences of characters separated by spaces (words). Each time the for loop executes, the value of the variable var is set to the next word in the list of words, word1 to wordN.

Example

Here is a simple example that uses the **for** loop to span through the given list of numbers –

```
#!/bin/sh


for var in 0 1 2 3 4 5 6 7 8 9

do

  echo $var

done
```

Upon execution, you will receive the following result −

```
0

1

2

3

4

5

6

7
```

8

9

Following is the example to display all the files starting with **.bash** and available in your home. We will execute this script from my root –

```
#!/bin/sh


for FILE in $HOME/.bash*

do

   echo $FILE

done
```

The above script will produce the following result –

```
/root/.bash_history

/root/.bash_logout

/root/.bash_profile

/root/.bashrc
```

- **The until loop**

The while loop is perfect for a situation where you need to execute a set of commands while some condition is true. Sometimes you need to execute a set of commands until a condition is true.

Syntax

```
until command

do

   Statement(s) to be executed until command is true

done
```

Here the Shell *command* is evaluated. If the resulting value is *false*, given *statement(s)* are executed. If the *command* is *true* then no statement will be executed and the program jumps to the next line after the done statement.

Example

Here is a simple example that uses the until loop to display the numbers zero to nine −

```
#!/bin/sh
```

```
a=0

until [ ! $a -lt 10 ]
do
   echo $a
   a=`expr $a + 1`
done
```

Upon execution, you will receive the following result −

```
0
1
2
3
4
5
6
7
```

8

9

- **The select loop**

The **select** loop provides an easy way to create a numbered menu from which users can select options. It is useful when you need to ask the user to choose one or more items from a list of choices.

Syntax

select var in word1 word2 ... wordN

do

Statement(s) to be executed for every word.

done

Here *var* is the name of a variable and **word1** to **wordN** are sequences of characters separated by spaces (words). Each time the **for** loop executes, the value of the variable var is set to the next word in the list of words, **word1** to **wordN**.

For every selection, a set of commands will be executed within the loop. This loop was introduced in **ksh** and has been adapted into bash. It is not available in **sh**.

Example

Here is a simple example to let the user select a drink of choice –

```
#!/bin/ksh

select DRINK in tea cofee water juice appe all none
do
   case $DRINK in
      tea|cofee|water|all)
         echo "Go to canteen"
         ;;
      juice|appe)
         echo "Available at home"
      ;;
      none)
         break
```

```
      ;;
      *) echo "ERROR: Invalid selection"
      ;;
   esac
done
```

The menu presented by the select loop looks like the following –

```
$./test.sh
1) tea
2) cofee
3) water
4) juice
5) appe
6) all
7) none
#? juice
```

Available at home

#? none

$

You can change the prompt displayed by the select loop by altering the variable PS3 as follows −

$PS3 = "Please make a selection => " ; export PS3

$./test.sh

1) tea

2) cofee

3) water

4) juice

5) appe

6) all

7) none

Please make a selection => juice

Available at home

Please make a selection => none

$

You will use different loops based on the situation. For example, the **while** loop executes the given commands until the given condition remains true; the **until** loop executes until a given condition becomes true.

Once you have good programming practice you will gain the expertise and thereby, start using appropriate loop based on the situation. Here, **while** and **for** loops are available in most of the other programming languages like **C**, **C++** and **PERL**, etc.

Nesting Loops

All the loops support nesting concept which means you can put one loop inside another similar one or different loops. This nesting can go up to unlimited number of times based on your requirement.

Here is an example of nesting **while** loop. The other loops can be nested based on the programming requirement in a similar way –

Nesting while Loops

It is possible to use a while loop as part of the body of another while loop.

Syntax

```
while command1 ; # this is loop1, the outer loop
do
   Statement(s) to be executed if command1 is true

   while command2 ; # this is loop2, the inner loop
   do
      Statement(s) to be executed if command2 is true
   done

   Statement(s) to be executed if command1 is true
done
```

Example

Here is a simple example of loop nesting. Let's add another countdown loop inside the loop that you used to count to nine −

```
#!/bin/sh


a=0

while [ "$a" -lt 10 ]    # this is loop1

do

   b="$a"

   while [ "$b" -ge 0 ]  # this is loop2

   do

      echo -n "$b "

      b=`expr $b - 1`

   done

   echo

   a=`expr $a + 1`

done
```

This will produce the following result. It is important to note how **echo -n** works here. Here **-n** option lets echo avoid printing a new line character.

```
0
1 0
2 1 0
3 2 1 0
4 3 2 1 0
5 4 3 2 1 0
6 5 4 3 2 1 0
7 6 5 4 3 2 1 0
8 7 6 5 4 3 2 1 0
9 8 7 6 5 4 3 2 1 0
```

8. Loop Control

In this chapter, we will discuss shell loop control in Unix. So far you have looked at creating loops and working with loops to accomplish different tasks. Sometimes you need to stop a loop or skip iterations of the loop.

In this chapter, we will learn following two statements that are used to control shell loops−

- The **break** statement
- The **continue** statement

The infinite Loop

All the loops have a limited life and they come out once the condition is false or true depending on the loop.

A loop may continue forever if the required condition is not met. A loop that executes forever without terminating executes for an infinite number of times. For this reason, such loops are called infinite loops.

Example

Here is a simple example that uses the **while** loop to display the numbers zero to nine −

```
#!/bin/sh


a=10



until [ $a -lt 10 ]

do

   echo $a

   a=`expr $a + 1`

done
```

This loop continues forever because **a** is always **greater than** or **equal to 10** and it is never less than 10.

The break Statement

The **break** statement is used to terminate the execution of the entire loop, after completing the execution of all of the lines of code up to the break statement. It then steps down to the code following the end of the loop.

Syntax

The following **break** statement is used to come out of a loop –

break

The break command can also be used to exit from a nested loop using this format –

break n

Here **n** specifies the $\mathbf{n}^{th}$ enclosing loop to the exit from.

Example

Here is a simple example which shows that loop terminates as soon as **a** becomes 5 –

```
#!/bin/sh


a=0


while [ $a -lt 10 ]

do
```

```
    echo $a
    if [ $a -eq 5 ]
    then
      break
    fi
    a=`expr $a + 1`
done
```

Upon execution, you will receive the following result −

```
0
1
2
3
4
5
```

Here is a simple example of nested for loop. This script breaks out of both loops if **var1 equals 2** and **var2 equals 0** −

```
#!/bin/sh


for var1 in 1 2 3

do

  for var2 in 0 5

  do

    if [ $var1 -eq 2 -a $var2 -eq 0 ]

    then

      break 2

    else

      echo "$var1 $var2"

    fi

  done

done
```

Upon execution, you will receive the following result. In the inner loop, you have a break command with the argument

2. This indicates that if a condition is met you should break out of outer loop and ultimately from the inner loop as well.

1 0

1 5

The continue statement

The **continue** statement is similar to the **break** command, except that it causes the current iteration of the loop to exit, rather than the entire loop.

This statement is useful when an error has occurred but you want to try to execute the next iteration of the loop.

Syntax

continue

Like with the break statement, an integer argument can be given to the continue command to skip commands from nested loops.

continue n

Here **n** specifies the **n**th enclosing loop to continue from.

Example

The following loop makes use of the **continue** statement which returns from the continue statement and starts processing the next statement –

```
#!/bin/sh

NUMS="1 2 3 4 5 6 7"

for NUM in $NUMS
do
  Q=`expr $NUM % 2`
  if [ $Q -eq 0 ]
  then
    echo "Number is an even number!!"
    continue
  fi
  echo "Found odd number"
done
```

Upon execution, you will receive the following result −

Found odd number

Number is an even number!!

Found odd number

Number is an even number!!

Found odd number

Number is an even number!!

Found odd number

9. Substitution

What is Substitution?

The shell performs substitution when it encounters an expression that contains one or more special characters.

Example

Here, the printing value of the variable is substituted by its value. Same time, **"\n"** is substituted by a new line –

```
#!/bin/sh


a=10

echo -e "Value of a is $a \n"
```

You will receive the following result. Here the **-e** option enables the interpretation of backslash escapes.

Value of a is 10

Following is the result without **-e** option –

Value of a is 10\n

The following escape sequences which can be used in echo command –

Sr.No.	Escape & Description
1	\\ backslash
2	**\a** alert (BEL)
3	**\b** backspace
4	**\c** suppress trailing newline
5	**\f** form feed
6	**\n** new line
7	**\r** carriage return
8	**\t** horizontal tab
9	**\v** vertical tab

You can use the **-E** option to disable the interpretation of the backslash escapes (default).

You can use the **-n** option to disable the insertion of a new line.

Command Substitution

Command substitution is the mechanism by which the shell performs a given set of commands and then substitutes their output in the place of the commands.

Syntax

The command substitution is performed when a command is given as –

`command`

When performing the command substitution make sure that you use the backquote, not the single quote character.

Example

Command substitution is generally used to assign the output of a command to a variable. Each of the following examples demonstrates the command substitution –

```
#!/bin/sh
```

```
DATE=`date`

echo "Date is $DATE"



USERS=`who | wc -l`

echo "Logged in user are $USERS"



UP=`date ; uptime`

echo "Uptime is $UP"
```

Upon execution, you will receive the following result −

Date is Thu Jul 2 03:59:57 MST 2009

Logged in user are 1

Uptime is Thu Jul 2 03:59:57 MST 2009

03:59:57 up 20 days, 14:03, 1 user, load avg: 0.13, 0.07, 0.15

Variable Substitution

Variable substitution enables the shell programmer to manipulate the value of a variable based on its state.

Here is the following table for all the possible substitutions −

Sr.No.	Form & Description
1	**${var}** Substitute the value of *var*.
2	**${var:-word}** If *var* is null or unset, *word* is substituted for **var**. The value of *var* does not change.
3	**${var:=word}** If *var* is null or unset, *var* is set to the value of **word**.
4	**${var:?message}** If *var* is null or unset, *message* is printed to standard error. This checks that variables are set correctly.
5	**${var:+word}** If *var* is set, *word* is substituted for var. The value of *var* does not change.

Example

Following is the example to show various states of the above substitution −

```
#!/bin/sh
```

```
echo ${var:-"Variable is not set"}

echo "1 - Value of var is ${var}"


echo ${var:="Variable is not set"}

echo "2 - Value of var is ${var}"


unset var

echo ${var:+"This is default value"}

echo "3 - Value of var is $var"


var="Prefix"

echo ${var:+"This is default value"}

echo "4 - Value of var is $var"


echo ${var:?"Print this message"}

echo "5 - Value of var is ${var}"
```

Upon execution, you will receive the following result –

Variable is not set

1 - Value of var is

Variable is not set

2 - Value of var is Variable is not set

3 - Value of var is

This is default value

4 - Value of var is Prefix

Prefix

5 - Value of var is Prefix

10. Quoting Mechanisms

In this chapter, we will discuss in detail about the Shell quoting mechanisms. We will start by discussing the metacharacters.

The Metacharacters

Unix Shell provides various metacharacters which have special meaning while using them in any Shell Script and causes termination of a word unless quoted.

For example, **?** matches with a single character while listing files in a directory and an * matches more than one character. Here is a list of most of the shell special characters (also called metacharacters) –

* ? [ ] ' " \ $; & ( ) | ^ < > new-line space tab

A character may be quoted (i.e., made to stand for itself) by preceding it with a \.

Example

Following example shows how to print a * or a **?** –

```
#!/bin/sh

echo Hello; Word
```

Upon execution, you will receive the following result –

Hello

./test.sh: line 2: Word: command not found

shell returned 127

Let us now try using a quoted character –

```
#!/bin/sh

echo Hello\; Word
```

Upon execution, you will receive the following result –

Hello; Word

The $ sign is one of the metacharacters, so it must be quoted to avoid special handling by the shell –

```
#!/bin/sh


echo "I have \$1200"
```

Upon execution, you will receive the following result –

I have $1200

The following table lists the four forms of quoting –

Sr.No.	Quoting & Description
1	**Single quote** All special characters between these quotes lose their special meaning.
2	**Double quote** Most special characters between these quotes lose their special meaning with these exceptions – $ ` \$

	\' \" \\
3	**Backslash** Any character immediately following the backslash loses its special meaning.
4	**Back quote** Anything in between back quotes would be treated as a command and would be executed.

The Single Quotes

Consider an echo command that contains many special shell characters –

```
echo <-$1500.**>; (update?) [y|n]
```

Putting a backslash in front of each special character is tedious and makes the line difficult to read –

```
echo \<-\$1500.\*\*\>\; \(update\?\) \[y\|n\]
```

There is an easy way to quote a large group of characters. Put a single quote (') at the beginning and at the end of the string –

```
echo '<-$1500.**>; (update?) [y|n]'
```

Characters within single quotes are quoted just as if a backslash is in front of each character. With this, the echo command displays in a proper way.

If a single quote appears within a string to be output, you should not put the whole string within single quotes instead you should precede that using a backslash (\) as follows –

echo 'It\'s Shell Programming

The Double Quotes

Try to execute the following shell script. This shell script makes use of single quote –

```
VAR=ZARA

echo '$VAR owes <-$1500.**>; [ as of (`date +%m/%d`) ]'
```

Upon execution, you will receive the following result –

$VAR owes <-$1500.**>; [as of (`date +%m/%d`)]

This is not what had to be displayed. It is obvious that single quotes prevent variable substitution. If you want to substitute variable values and to make inverted commas work as expected, then you would need to put your commands in double quotes as follows –

```
VAR=ZARA
```

```
echo "$VAR owes <-\$1500.**>; [ as of (`date +%m/%d`) ]"
```

Upon execution, you will receive the following result –

```
ZARA owes <-$1500.**>; [ as of (07/02) ]
```

Double quotes take away the special meaning of all characters except the following –

- **$** for parameter substitution
- Backquotes for command substitution
- **\$** to enable literal dollar signs
- \` to enable literal backquotes
- \" to enable embedded double quotes
- \\ to enable embedded backslashes
- All other \ characters are literal (not special)

Characters within single quotes are quoted just as if a backslash is in front of each character. This helps the echo command display properly.

If a single quote appears within a string to be output, you should not put the whole string within single quotes instead you should precede that using a backslash (\) as follows –

```
echo 'It\'s Shell Programming'
```

The Backquotes

Putting any Shell command in between **backquotes** executes the command.

Syntax

Here is the simple syntax to put any Shell **command** in between backquotes –

var=`command`

Example

The **date** command is executed in the following example and the produced result is stored in DATA variable.

```
DATE=`date`


echo "Current Date: $DATE"
```

Upon execution, you will receive the following result –

Current Date: Thu Jul 2 05:28:45 MST 2009

11. Input/Output Redirections

In this chapter, we will discuss in detail about the Shell input/output redirections. Most Unix system commands take input from your terminal and send the resulting output back to your terminal. A command normally reads its input from the standard input, which happens to be your terminal by default. Similarly, a command normally writes its output to standard output, which is again your terminal by default.

Output Redirection

The output from a command normally intended for standard output can be easily diverted to a file instead. This capability is known as output redirection.

If the notation > file is appended to any command that normally writes its output to standard output, the output of that command will be written to file instead of your terminal.

Check the following **who** command which redirects the complete output of the command in the users file.

```
$ who > users
```

Notice that no output appears at the terminal. This is because the output has been redirected from the default standard output device (the terminal) into the specified file. You can check the users file for the complete content –

```
$ cat users

oko      tty01   Sep 12 07:30

ai       tty15   Sep 12 13:32

ruth     tty21   Sep 12 10:10

pat      tty24   Sep 12 13:07

steve    tty25   Sep 12 13:03

$
```

If a command has its output redirected to a file and the file already contains some data, that data will be lost. Consider the following example –

```
$ echo line 1 > users

$ cat users

line 1

$
```

You can use >> operator to append the output in an existing file as follows –

$ echo line 2 >> users

$ cat users

line 1

line 2

$

Input Redirection

Just as the output of a command can be redirected to a file, so can the input of a command be redirected from a file. As the **greater-than character >** is used for output redirection, the **less-than character <** is used to redirect the input of a command.

The commands that normally take their input from the standard input can have their input redirected from a file in this manner. For example, to count the number of lines in the file *users* generated above, you can execute the command as follows –

$ wc -l users

2 users

$

Upon execution, you will receive the following output. You can count the number of lines in the file by redirecting the standard input of the **wc** command from the file *users* –

$ wc -l < users

2

$

Note that there is a difference in the output produced by the two forms of the wc command. In the first case, the name of the file users is listed with the line count; in the second case, it is not.

In the first case, wc knows that it is reading its input from the file users. In the second case, it only knows that it is reading its input from standard input so it does not display file name.

Here Document

A **here document** is used to redirect input into an interactive shell script or program.

We can run an interactive program within a shell script without user action by supplying the required input for the interactive program, or interactive shell script.

The general form for a **here** document is –

```
command << delimiter

document

delimiter
```

Here the shell interprets the **<<** operator as an instruction to read input until it finds a line containing the specified delimiter. All the input lines up to the line containing the delimiter are then fed into the standard input of the command.

The delimiter tells the shell that the **here** document has completed. Without it, the shell continues to read the input forever. The delimiter must be a single word that does not contain spaces or tabs.

Following is the input to the command **wc -l** to count the total number of lines −

```
$wc -l << EOF
   This is a simple lookup program
        for good (and bad) restaurants
        in Cape Town.
EOF
3
```

```
$
```

You can use the **here document** to print multiple lines using your script as follows –

```
#!/bin/sh

cat << EOF
This is a simple lookup program
for good (and bad) restaurants
in Cape Town.
EOF
```

Upon execution, you will receive the following result –

This is a simple lookup program

for good (and bad) restaurants

in Cape Town.

The following script runs a session with the **vi** text editor and saves the input in the file **test.txt**.

```
#!/bin/sh

filename=test.txt
vi $filename <<EndOfCommands
i
This file was created automatically from
a shell script
^[
ZZ
EndOfCommands
```

If you run this script with vim acting as vi, then you will likely see output like the following −

```
$ sh test.sh
Vim: Warning: Input is not from a terminal
$
```

After running the script, you should see the following added to the file **test.txt** −

```
$ cat test.txt

This file was created automatically from

a shell script

$
```

Discard the output

Sometimes you will need to execute a command, but you don't want the output displayed on the screen. In such cases, you can discard the output by redirecting it to the file **/dev/null** −

```
$ command > /dev/null
```

Here command is the name of the command you want to execute. The file **/dev/null** is a special file that automatically discards all its input.

To discard both output of a command and its error output, use standard redirection to redirect **STDERR** to **STDOUT** −

```
$ command > /dev/null 2>&1
```

Here **2** represents **STDERR** and **1** represents **STDOUT**. You can display a message on to STDERR by redirecting STDOUT into STDERR as follows −

```
$ echo message 1>&2
```

Redirection Commands

Following is a complete list of commands which you can use for redirection –

Sr.No.	Command & Description
1	**pgm > file** Output of pgm is redirected to file
2	**pgm < file** Program pgm reads its input from file
3	**pgm >> file** Output of pgm is appended to file
4	**n > file** Output from stream with descriptor **n** redirected to file
5	**n >> file** Output from stream with descriptor **n** appended to file
6	**n >& m** Merges output from stream **n** with stream **m**
7	**n <& m** Merges input from stream **n** with stream **m**
8	**<< tag** Standard input comes from here through next tag at the start of line
9	| Takes output from one program, or process, and sends it to another

Note that the file descriptor **0** is normally standard input (STDIN), **1** is standard output (STDOUT), and **2** is standard error output (STDERR)

12. Shell Functions

In this chapter, we will discuss in detail about the shell functions. Functions enable you to break down the overall functionality of a script into smaller, logical subsections, which can then be called upon to perform their individual tasks when needed.

Using functions to perform repetitive tasks is an excellent way to create **code reuse**. This is an important part of modern object-oriented programming principles.

Shell functions are similar to subroutines, procedures, and functions in other programming languages.

Creating Functions

To declare a function, simply use the following syntax –

```
function_name () {

   list of commands

}
```

The name of your function is **function_name**, and that's what you will use to call it from elsewhere in your scripts.

The function name must be followed by parentheses, followed by a list of commands enclosed within braces.

Example

Following example shows the use of function –

```
#!/bin/sh

# Define your function here
Hello () {
   echo "Hello World"
}

# Invoke your function
Hello
```

Upon execution, you will receive the following output –

$./test.sh

Hello World

Pass Parameters to a Function

You can define a function that will accept parameters while calling the function. These parameters would be represented by **$1**, **$2** and so on.

Following is an example where we pass two parameters *Zara* and *Ali* and then we capture and print these parameters in the function.

```
#!/bin/sh

# Define your function here
Hello () {
  echo "Hello World $1 $2"
}

# Invoke your function
Hello Zara Ali
```

Upon execution, you will receive the following result –

```
$./test.sh
```

Hello World Zara Ali

Returning Values from Functions

If you execute an **exit** command from inside a function, its effect is not only to terminate execution of the function but also of the shell program that called the function.

If you instead want to just terminate execution of the function, then there is way to come out of a defined function.

Based on the situation you can return any value from your function using the **return** command whose syntax is as follows −

return code

Here **code** can be anything you choose here, but obviously you should choose something that is meaningful or useful in the context of your script as a whole.

Example

Following function returns a value 10 −

```
#!/bin/sh


# Define your function here
```

```
Hello () {
  echo "Hello World $1 $2"
  return 10
}

# Invoke your function
Hello Zara Ali

# Capture value returnd by last command
ret=$?

echo "Return value is $ret"
```

Upon execution, you will receive the following result –

```
$./test.sh
Hello World Zara Ali
Return value is 10
```

Nested Functions

One of the more interesting features of functions is that they can call themselves and also other functions. A function that calls itself is known as a ***recursive function***.

Following example demonstrates nesting of two functions −

```
#!/bin/sh


# Calling one function from another

number_one () {

   echo "This is the first function speaking..."

   number_two

}


number_two () {

   echo "This is now the second function speaking..."

}
```

```
# Calling function one.
number_one
```

Upon execution, you will receive the following result −

```
This is the first function speaking...
This is now the second function speaking...
```

Function Call from Prompt

You can put definitions for commonly used functions inside your ***.profile***. These definitions will be available whenever you log in and you can use them at the command prompt.

Alternatively, you can group the definitions in a file, say ***test.sh***, and then execute the file in the current shell by typing −

```
$. test.sh
```

This has the effect of causing functions defined inside ***test.sh*** to be read and defined to the current shell as follows −

```
$ number_one
This is the first function speaking...
```

This is now the second function speaking...

$

To remove the definition of a function from the shell, use the unset command with the **.f** option. This command is also used to remove the definition of a variable to the shell.

```
$ unset -f function_name
```

13. Manpage Help

All the Unix commands come with a number of optional and mandatory options. It is very common to forget the complete syntax of these commands.

Because no one can possibly remember every Unix command and all its options, we have online help available to mitigate this right from when Unix was at its development stage.

Unix's version of **Help files** are called **man pages**. If there is a command name and you are not sure how to use it, then Man Pages help you out with every step.

Syntax

Here is the simple command that helps you get the detail of any Unix command while working with the system −

```
$man command
```

Example

Suppose there is a command that requires you to get help; assume that you want to know about **pwd** then you simply need to use the following command −

```
$man pwd
```

The above command helps you with the complete information about the **pwd** command. Try it yourself at your command prompt to get more detail.

You can get complete detail on **man** command itself using the following command –

$man man

Man Page Sections

Man pages are generally divided into sections, which generally vary by the man page author's preference. Following table lists some common sections –

Sr.No.	Section & Description
1	**NAME** Name of the command
2	**SYNOPSIS** General usage parameters of the command
3	**DESCRIPTION** Describes what the command does
4	**OPTIONS** Describes all the arguments or options to the command
5	**SEE ALSO** Lists other commands that are directly related to the command in the man page or closely resemble its functionality
6	**BUGS** Explains any known issues or bugs that exist with the command or its output
7	**EXAMPLES** Common usage examples that give the reader an idea of how the command can be used
8	**AUTHORS**

	The author of the man page/command

To sum it up, man pages are a vital resource and the first avenue of research when you need information about commands or files in a Unix system.

Useful Shell Commands

The following link gives you a list of the most important and very frequently used Unix Shell commands.

If you do not know how to use any command, then use man page to get complete detail about the command.

Here is the list of **Unix Shell - Useful Commands**

This quick guide lists commands, including a syntax and a brief description. For more detail, use −

$man command

Files and Directories

These commands allow you to create directories and handle files.

Given below is the list of commands in Files and Directories.

Manipulating data

The contents of files can be compared and altered with the following commands.

Given below is the list of commands in Manipulating data.

Compressed Files

Files may be compressed to save space. Compressed files can be created and examined.

Sr.No.	Command & Description
1	**compress** Compresses files
2	**gunzip** Helps uncompress gzipped files
3	**gzip** GNU alternative compression method
4	**uncompress** Helps uncompress files
5	**unzip** List, test and extract compressed files in a ZIP archive
6	**zcat** Cat a compressed file
7	**zcmp** Compares compressed files
8	**zdiff** Compares compressed files
9	**zmore** File perusal filter for crt viewing of compressed text

Getting Information

Various Unix manuals and documentation are available on-line. The following Shell commands give information −

Sr.No.	Command & Description
1	**apropos** Locates commands by keyword lookup
2	**info** Displays command information pages online
2	**man** Displays manual pages online
3	**whatis** Searches the whatis database for complete words
4	**yelp** GNOME help viewer

Network Communication

These following commands are used to send and receive files from a local Unix hosts to the remote host around the world.

Sr.No.	Command & Description
1	**ftp** File transfer program
2	**rcp** Remote file copy
3	**rlogin** Remote login to a Unix host
4	**rsh**

	Remote shell
5	**tftp** Trivial file transfer program
6	**telnet** Makes terminal connection to another host
7	**ssh** Secures shell terminal or command connection
8	**scp** Secures shell remote file copy
9	**sftp** Secures shell file transfer program

Some of these commands may be restricted at your computer for security reasons.

Messages between Users

The Unix systems support on-screen messages to other users and world-wide electronic mail −

Sr.No.	Command & Description
1	**evolution** GUI mail handling tool on Linux
2	**mail** Simple send or read mail program
3	**mesg** Permits or denies messages
4	**parcel** Sends files to another user
5	**pine** Vdu-based mail utility
6	**talk** Talks to another user

7	**write** Writes message to another user

Programming Utilities

The following programming tools and languages are available based on what you have installed on your Unix.

Given below is the list of tools and languages in Programming Utilities.

Misc Commands

These commands list or alter information about the system –

Given below is the list of Misc Commands in Unix.

Sr.No.	Command & Description
1	**chfn** Changes your finger information
2	**chgrp** Changes the group ownership of a file
3	**chown** Changes owner
4	**date** Prints the date
5	**determin**

	Automatically finds terminal type
6	**du** Prints amount of disk usage
7	**echo** Echo arguments to the standard options
8	**exit** Quits the system
9	**finger** Prints information about logged-in users
10	**groupadd** Creates a user group
11	**groups** Show group memberships
12	**homequota** Shows quota and file usage
13	**iostat** Reports I/O statistics
14	**kill** Sends a signal to a process
15	**last** Shows last logins of users
16	**logout**

	Logs off Unix
17	**lun** Lists user names or login ID
18	**netstat** Shows network status
19	**passwd** Changes user password
20	**passwd** Changes your login password
21	**printenv** Displays value of a shell variable
22	**ps** Displays the status of current processes
23	**ps** Prints process status statistics
24	**quota -v** Displays disk usage and limits
25	**reset** Resets terminal mode
26	**script** Keeps script of terminal session
27	**script**

	Saves the output of a command or process
28	**setenv** Sets environment variables
30	**stty** Sets terminal options
31	**time** Helps time a command
32	**top** Displays all system processes
33	**tset** Sets terminal mode
34	**tty** Prints current terminal name
35	**umask** Show the permissions that are given to view files by default
36	**uname** Displays name of the current system
37	**uptime** Gets the system up time
38	**useradd** Creates a user account

39	**users** Prints names of logged in users
40	**vmstat** Reports virtual memory statistics
41	**w** Shows what logged in users are doing
42	**who** Lists logged in users

14. Builtin Mathematical Functions

The most of the part of this tutorial covered Bourne Shell but this page list down all the mathematical builti-in functions available in **Korn** Shell.

The Korn shell provides access to the standard set of mathematical functions. They are called using C function call syntax.

Sr.No.	Function & Description
1	**abs** Absolute value
2	**log** Natural logarithm
3	**acos** Arc cosine
4	**sin** Sine
5	**asin** Arc sine
6	**sinh** Hyperbolic sine
7	**cos** Cosine

8	**sqrt** Square root
9	**cosh** Hyperbolic cosine
10	**tan** Tangent
11	**exp** Exponential function
12	**tanh** Hyperbolic tangent
13	**int** Integer part of floating-point number

Reference Books:-

- **"Learning the bash Shell"** by Cameron Newham and Bill Rosenblatt, O'Reilly Media, 2005.
- **"Classic Shell Scripting"** by Arnold Robbins and Nelson H.F. Beebe, O'Reilly Media, 2005.
- **"Bash Cookbook"** by Carl Albing, JP Vossen, and Cameron Newham, O'Reilly Media, 2007.
- **"Pro Bash Programming: Scripting the GNU/Linux Shell"** by Chris F.A. Johnson and Jayant Varma, Apress, 2009.
- **"Linux Command Line and Shell Scripting Bible"** by Richard Blum and Christine Bresnahan, Wiley, 2021.

www.ingramcontent.com/pod-product-compliance
Lightning Source LLC
LaVergne TN
LVHW010609160826
845677LV00013B/3323

* 9 7 9 8 8 9 5 4 4 9 6 2 2 *